PUFFIN BOOKS

Editor: Kaye Webb

SILLY VERSE FOR KIDS

PUFFIN BOOKS

SILLY VERSE FOR KIDS

SPIKE MILLIGAN

Puffin Books: a Division of Penguin Books Ltd, Harmondsworth,
Middlesex, England
Penguin Books Australia Ltd, Ringwood, Victoria, Australia

—

Contents of this volume first published by Dennis Dobson in *Silly Verse for Kids*,
A Dustbin of Milligan and *The Pot Boiler*
1959, 1961, 1963

—

Published in Puffin Books 1968
Reprinted 1968 (twice), 1970, 1971, 1972, 1973 (twice), 1974

—

Copyright © Spike Milligan 1959, 1961, 1963

—

The poems on pp. 61–71 are printed by permission of
Tandem Books

—

Made and printed in Great Britain by
Cox & Wyman Ltd, London, Reading and Fakenham
Set in Monotype Joanna

This book
is dedicated to
my bank balance

Contents

Foreword

Most of these poems were written to amuse my children; some were written as the result of things they said in the home. No matter what you say, my kids think I'm brilliant.

S. M.

String

String
Is a very important thing.
Rope is thicker,
But string,
Is quicker.

P.S. The meaning of this is obscure
That's why, the higher the fewer.

Mary Pugh

Mary Pugh
Was nearly two
When she went out of doors.
She went out standing up she did
But came back on all fours.
The moral of the story
Please meditate and pause:
Never send a baby out
With loosely waisted draws.

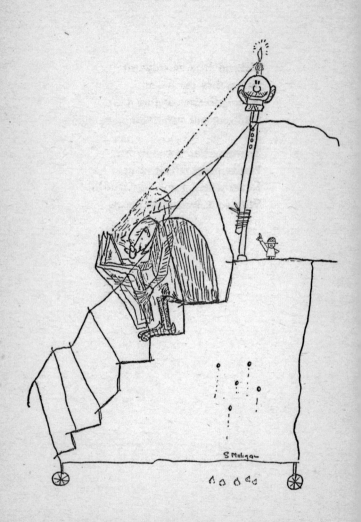

S Milligan

Tell me little woodworm

Tell me little woodworm
Eating thru the wood.
Surely all that sawdust
Can't do you any good.

Heavens! Little woodworm
You've eaten all the chairs
So *that's* why poor old Grandad's
Sitting outside on the stairs.

Hipporhinostricow

Such a beast is the Hipporhinostricow
How it got so mixed up we'll never know how;
It sleeps all day, and whistles all night,
And it wears yellow socks which are far too tight.

If you laugh at the Hipporhinostricow,
You're bound to get into an awful row;
The creature is protected you see
From silly people like you and me.

I've never felt finer

'I've never felt finer!'
Said the King of China,
Sitting down to dine –
Then fell down dead – he died he did!
It was only half past nine.

Said the General

Said the General of the Army,
'I think that war is barmy'
So he threw away his gun:
Now he's having much more fun.

Two children (small)

Two children (small), one Four, one Five,
Once saw a bee go in a hive.
They'd never seen a bee before!
So waited there to see some more.
And sure enough along there came
A dozen bees (and all the same!)
Within the hive they buzzed about;
Then, one by one, they all flew out.
Said Four: 'Those bees *are* silly things,
But how I wish I *had* their wings!'

Granny

Through every nook and every cranny
The wind blew in on poor old Granny;
Around her knees, into each ear
(And up her nose as well, I fear).

All through the night the wind grew worse,
It nearly made the vicar curse.
The top had fallen off the steeple
Just missing him (and other people).

It blew on man; it blew on beast.
It blew on nun; it blew on priest.
It blew the wig off Auntie Fanny —
But most of all, it blew on Granny! !

Hello Jolly Guardsman

'Hello Jolly Guardsman
In your scarlet coat:
It reaches from below your tum
To half way up your throat.

'Tell me jolly Guardsman
When you're off parade
What kind of clothes do you put on?'
'Civvies I'm afraid.'

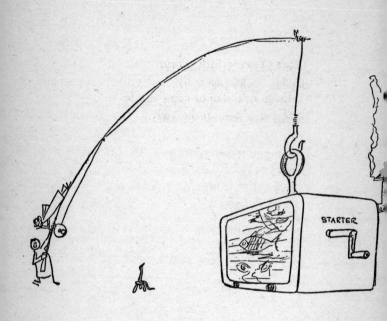

Today I saw a little worm

Today I saw a little worm
Wriggling on his belly.
Perhaps he'd like to come inside
And see what's on the Telly.

Teeth

English Teeth, English Teeth!
Shining in the sun
A part of British heritage
Aye, each and every one.

English Teeth, Happy Teeth!
Always having fun
Clamping down on bits of fish
And sausages half done.

English Teeth! HEROES' Teeth!
Hear them click! and clack!
Let's sing a song of praise to them —
Three Cheers for the Brown Grey and Black.

Look at all those monkeys

Look at all those monkeys
Jumping in their cage.
Why don't they all go out to work
And earn a decent wage?

> How can you say such silly things,
> And you a son of mine?
> Imagine monkeys travelling on
> The Morden—Edgware line!

But what about the Pekinese!
They have an allocation.
'Don't travel during Peke hour',
It says on every station.

> My Gosh, you're right, my clever boy,
> I never thought of that!
> And so they left the monkey house,
> While an elephant raised his hat.

Can a parrot

Can a parrot
Eat a carrot
Standing on his head?
If I did that my mum would send me
Straight upstairs to bed.

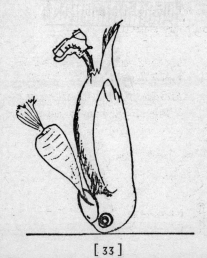

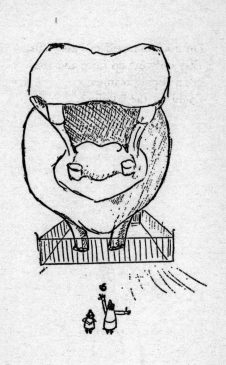

I'm not frightened of Pussy Cats

I'm not frightened of Pussy Cats,
They only eat up mice and rats,
But a Hippopotamus
Could eat the Lotofus!

Down the stream the swans all glide

Down the stream the swans all glide;
It's quite the cheapest way to ride.
Their legs get wet,
Their tummies wetter:
I think after all
The bus is better.

On the Ning Nang Nong

On the Ning Nang Nong
Where the Cows go Bong!
And the Monkeys all say Boo!
There's a Nong Nang Ning
Where the trees go Ping!
And the tea pots Jibber Jabber Joo.
On the Nong Ning Nang
All the mice go Clang!
And you just can't catch 'em when they do!
So it's Ning Nang Nong!
Cows go Bong!
Nong Nang Ning!
Trees go Ping!
Nong Ning Nang!
The mice go Clang!
What a noisy place to belong,
Is the Ning Nang Ning Nang Nong! !

The Land of the Bumbley Boo

In the Land of the Bumbley Boo
The people are red white and blue,
They never blow noses,
Or ever wear closes,
What a sensible thing to do!

In the Land of the Bumbley Boo
You can buy Lemon pie at the Zoo;
They give away Foxes
In little Pink Boxes
And Bottles of Dandylion Stew.

In the Land of the Bumbley Boo
You never see a Gnu,
But thousands of cats
Wearing trousers and hats
Made of Pumpkins and Pelican Glue!

Chorus

Oh, the Bumbley Boo! the Bumbley Boo!
That's the place for me and you!
So hurry! Let's run!
The train leaves at one!
For the Land of the Bumbley Boo!
The wonderful Bumbley Boo-Boo-Boo!
The Wonderful Bumbley BOO!!!

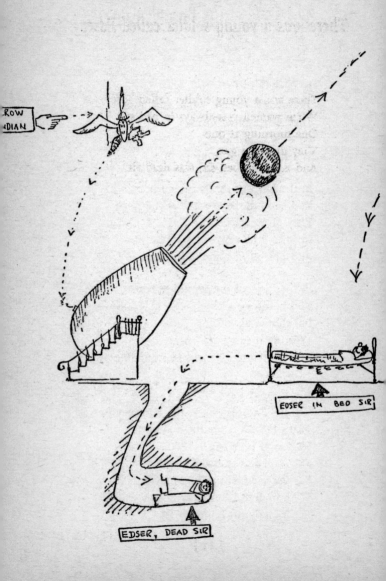

There was a young soldier called Edser

There was a young soldier called Edser
When wanted was always in bed sir:
One morning at one
They fired the gun
And Edser, in bed sir, was dead sir.

You must never bath in an Irish Stew

You must never bath in an Irish Stew
It's a most illogical thing to do
    But should you persist against my reasoning
    Don't fail to add the appropriate seasoning.

Hello Mr Python

Hello Mr Python
Curling round a tree,
Bet you'd like to make yourself
A dinner out of me.

Can't you change your habits
Crushing people's bones?
I wouldn't like a dinner
That emitted fearful groans.

A thousand hairy savages

A thousand hairy savages
Sitting down to lunch
Gobble gobble glup glup
Munch munch munch.

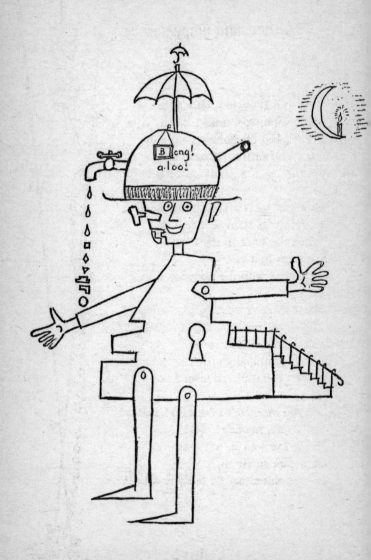

The Bongaloo

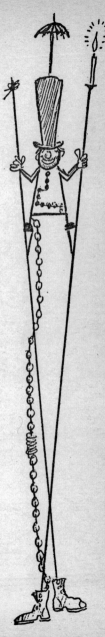

'What is a Bongaloo, Daddy?'
'A Bongaloo, Son,' said I,
'Is a tall bag of cheese
Plus a Chinaman's knees
And the leg of a nanny goat's eye.'

'How strange is a Bongaloo, Daddy?'
'As strange as strange,' I replied.
'When the sun's in the West
It appears in a vest
Sailing out with the noonday tide.'

'What shape is a Bongaloo, Daddy?'
'The shape, my Son, I'll explain:
It's tall round the nose
Which continually grows
In the general direction of Spain.'

'Are you sure there's a Bongaloo, Daddy?'
'Am I sure, my Son?' said I.
'Why, I've seen it, not quite
On a dark sunny night
Do you think that I'd tell you a lie?'

My sister Laura

My sister Laura's bigger than me
And lifts me up quite easily.
I can't lift her, I've tried and tried;
She must have something heavy inside.

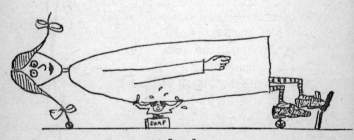

Failure

I'm trying to write the longest first line that poetry has ever had,
For a start that wasn't bad,
Now here comes a longer oneeeeeeeeeeeeeeeeeeeeeeeeeeeeeeeeeeeeeeeeeeeeeeeeeeee
I know I cheated:
It was the only way I could avoid being defeated.

I once knew a Burmese horse

I once knew a Burmese horse:
Of course
He didn't know he was a horse;
But I knew Jim
So I told him –
Now he knows
And so, I close.

My daddy wears a big black hat

My daddy wears a big black hat;
He wears it in the street
And raises it to lady folk
That he perchance should meet.
He wears it on a Sunday
And on a Monday too.
He never wears it in the house,
But only out of doors.

Maveric

Maveric Prowles
Had Rumbling Bowles
That thundered in the night.
It shook the bedrooms all around
And gave the folks a fright.

The doctor called;
He was appalled
When through his stethoscope
He heard the sound of a baying hound,
And the acrid smell of smoke.

Was there a cure?
'The higher the fewer,'
The learned doctor said,
Then turned poor Maveric inside out
And stood him on his head.

'Just as I thought
You've been and caught
An Asiatic flu –
You musn't go near dogs I fear
Unless they come near you.'

Poor Maveric cried.
He went cross-eyed,
His legs went green and blue.
The doctor hit him with a club
And charged him one and two.

And so my friend
This is the end,
A warning to the few:
Stay clear of doctors to **the end**
Or they'll get rid of **you**.

Confined-to-bed Elephant

Contagion

Elephants are contagious!
  Be careful how you tread.
An Elephant that's been trodden on
  Should be confined to bed!

Leopards are contagious too.
  Be careful tiny tots.
They don't give you a temperature
  But lots and lots — of spots.

The Herring is a lucky fish,
  From all disease inured.
Should he be ill when caught at sea;
  Immediately — he's cured!

Round and Round

Small poem based upon my daughter's (6) remarks on overhearing me tell her brother Sean (4½) that the world was going round. (Australia, June–July, 1958.)

One day a little boy called Sean
(Age four) became profound.
He asked his dad
If it were true
The world was going round.

'Oh yes, that's true,' his daddy said.
'It goes round night and day.'
'Then doesn't it get tired dad?'
Young Sean was heard to say.

His sister in the bath called out
'What did dad say – what did he?'
He said 'The world is going round.'
Said she 'Well it's making me giddy!'

The ABC

T'was midnight in the schoolroom
And every desk was shut,
When suddenly from the alphabet
Was heard a loud 'Tut-tut!'

Said A to B, 'I don't like C;
His manners are a lack.
For all I ever see of C
Is a semi-circular back!'

'I disagree,' said D to B,
'I've never found C so.
From where I stand, he seems to be
An uncompleted O.'

C was vexed, 'I'm much perplexed,
You criticize my shape.
I'm made like that, to help spell Cat
And Cow and Cool and Cape.'

'He's right,' said E; said F, 'Whoopee!'
Said G, ''Ip, 'ip, 'ooray!'
'You're dropping me,' roared H to G.
'Don't do it please I pray!'

'Out of my way,' LL said to K.
'I'll make poor I look ILL.'
To stop this stunt, J stood in front,
And presto! ILL was JILL.

'U know,' said V, 'that W
Is twice the age of me,
For as a Roman V is five
I'm half as young as he.'

X and Y yawned sleepily,
'Look at the time!' they said.
'Let's all get off to beddy byes.'
They did, then, 'Z-z-z.'

or

alternative last verse

X and Y yawned sleepily,
'Look at the time!' they said.
They all jumped in to beddy byes
And the last one in was Z!

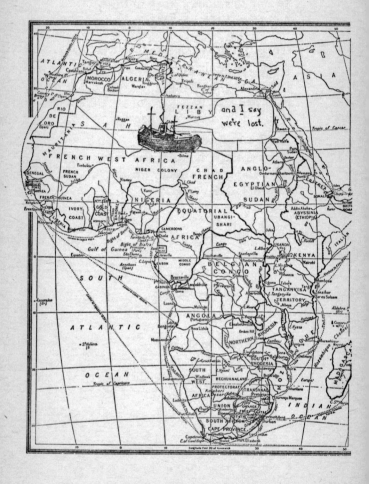

Bump!

Things that go 'bump!' in the night,
Should not really give one a fright.
It's the hole in each ear
That lets in the fear,
That, and the absence of light!

Soldier Freddy
          was never ready,
But Soldier Neddy,
          unlike Freddy,
Was always ready
          and steady,

Thats why,
When soldier Neddy
Is·outside·Buckingham·Palace·on·guard·in·the·
               pouring·wind·and·rain·
               being·steady·and·ready,
          Freddie —
               is home in beddy

NOTHING.

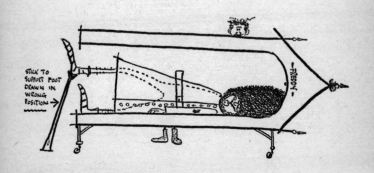

STICK TO
SUPPORT FOOT
DRAWN IN
WRONG
POSITION →

Rain

There are holes in the sky
    Where the rain gets in,
But they're ever so small
    That's why rain is thin.

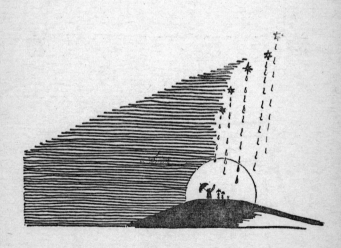

Some more humour in Puffins

SELECTED CAUTIONARY VERSES

Hilaire Belloc

This revised collection of the best of Belloc contains a number of his superbly funny cautionary tales in verse and some useful observations on animal behaviour. With the original drawings by B.T.B. and Nicolas Bentley.

PROFESSOR BRANESTAWM'S TREASURE HUNT

Norman Hunter

When it was a case of inventing an unspillable teacup, a collapsible-cum-expandable house, a liquid carpet to be applied with a brush, a machine for peeling and pipping grapes, a bomb or a fire alarm, Professor Branestawm was the man for the job. His interests were wide, and his intentions excellent, but it simply isn't any joke to be an inventor, or to be anywhere near one, as the Professor's military friend Colonel Dedshott and his long-suffering housekeeper Mrs Flittersnoop well knew.

Readers who first met this eccentric genius in *The Incredible Adventures of Professor Branestawm* will find the new adventures in his book just as hilariously impossible.

SPIDERWEB FOR TWO

Elizabeth Enright

'This is going to be the worst winter in my life,' said Randy Melendy. She said it because the older ones had all gone away to school, and the house was terribly tidy and quiet with just her, Oliver, and Cuffy their housekeeper.

Then a mysterious envelope arrived and inside it was the first clue in a truly marvellous treasure hunt. It seemed as if somebody had guessed how miserable they would be on their own, but who could it be who wrote the clues, and who knew so many wonderful hiding places in their own home? Rush? Father? Still, they did enjoy the strange adventures that grew out of it – and when they found the treasure it was the biggest surprise of all. By the author of The Saturdays, The Four-Storey Mistake and Then There were Five.

A PONY IN THE LUGGAGE

Gunnel Linde

It all began when Aunt Tina insisted on taking her nephew and niece on a trip to Copenhagen. And she managed splendidly, even when Nicholas helped an old gentleman off the train with two suitcases belonging to someone else, and the children developed their eccentric passion for visiting the zoo. (How could she guess that they intended to win a pony in a lottery?) Even at the hotel, when people in the room below began complaining of stamping and jumping noises on the ceiling, she didn't guess that there really was a pony in the children's bedroom, or that they were planning to keep it hidden from her until they got it safely home.

A hilarious story by a prizewinning Swedish author which keeps you laughing and wondering to the very end. For readers of eight and over, whether they love ponies or not.

THE DAY THE CEILING FELL DOWN

Jenifer Wayne

One hot exhausting summer day Louisa, Japhet and Rose, and their mother, came home to find a tramp in the kitchen and a hole in the bedroom ceiling. They found newspapers in the rubble of the ceiling which set them searching for the last tenant of their house, a blind old sea captain who had been unjustly turned out. A water main burst, someone was lost, the garden roller fell into a well, and someone shot the television.

This is a funny happy book which you will remember for a long time. For readers of nine and over.

BULLWHIP GRIFFIN

Sid Fleischman

It was 1849, the height of the California Gold Rush, when young Jack Flagg stowed away on a ship bound for San Francisco. His plan was to discover gold and so restore the fortunes of his Aunt Arabella, but he would have fared badly if it had not been for Praiseworthy, the remarkable butler who also turned out to be a dab hand at catching thieves, stoking boilers, cutting hair, and panning gold. He also vanquishes a particularly tough villain without even taking off his impeccable white gloves.

A funny, exciting and unusual story, which was recently filmed by Walt Disney.

MIDNITE

Randolph Stow

Midnite was not very bright and when he became an orphan his animal friends decided he should be a bushranger, but he wasn't very good at that either. He robbed a judge, and Trooper O'Grady robbed him.

A funny and unusual book, for readers of nine and over.

HOW TO BE TOPP

Geoffrey Willans and Ronald Searle

It is only fair to admit that Nigel Molesworth, the Curse of St Custards, is not everybody's favourite character. There are masters who ban his presence in the school library, or cite him as an Awful Warning to their pupils, and there are parents who condemn his manners and his spelling as a disgrace to the noble name of Education. But there are also parents, the kind who treasure their children's first letters, who find him irresistible, and masters who use him as a valuable guide in the strange labyrinth of a Schoolboy's Mind.

A book for everyone over nine who wants to laugh and knows how to spell.

If you have enjoyed this book and would like to know about others which we publish, why not join the Puffin Club? You will receive the Club magazine, Puffin Post, four times a year and a smart badge and membership book. You will also be able to enter all the competitions. For details, send a stamped addressed envelope to:

The Puffin Club Dept. A
Penguin Books Limited
Bath Road
Harmondsworth
Middlesex